INTERNET
ANIMAL
STARS

RACCOONS UNITE

REBECCA FELIX

Lerner Publications ◆ Minneapolis

Lerner Publications Company
An imprint of Lerner Publishing Group, Inc.
241 First Avenue North
Minneapolis, MN 55401 USA

For reading levels and more information, look up this title at www.lernerbooks.com.
Main body text set in Caecilia Com
Typeface provided by Monotype

Library of Congress Cataloging-in-Publication Data

Names: Felix, Rebecca, 1984– author.
Title: Raccoons unite / Rebecca Felix.
Description: Minneapolis : Lerner Publications, [2021] | Series: Internet animal stars | Includes bibliographical references and index. | Audience: Ages 6–10 | Audience: Grades 2–3 | Summary: "Raccoons look like little outlaws but they are perfectly at home on the internet! This title gives young readers info about the raccoon life cycle and habitat, and engages them with a clever social-media-inspired design"— Provided by publisher.
Identifiers: LCCN 2019058504 (print) | LCCN 2019058505 (ebook) | ISBN 9781541597143 (library binding) | ISBN 9781728402918 (paperback) | ISBN 9781728400396 (ebook)
Subjects: LCSH: Raccoon—Juvenile literature.
Classification: LCC QL737.C26 F45 2021 (print) | LCC QL737.C26 (ebook) | DDC 599.76/32—dc23

LC record available at https://lccn.loc.gov/2019058468
LC ebook record available at https://lccn.loc.gov/2019058469

Manufactured in the United States of America
1 – CG – 7/15/20

#Raccool

PAGE PLUS

Scan QR codes throughout the book for videos of cute animals!

RACCOONS UNITE

What do you know about raccoons? These masked mammals are related to bears. But they are much smaller! Raccoons are clever. Their **antics** entertain humans.

#RaccoonRace
Raccoons can run up to 15 miles (24 km) per hour!

The internet is filled with cute raccoon **content**. Learn basic facts about these furry animals. Then discover how raccoons became social media stars!

#RaccStar

Chapter 1

LITTERS & LIFESPAN

★ Little Kits ★

Baby raccoons are called kits. They have dark coats and a dark mask around their eyes. This mask remains visible throughout their lives.

Kits stand at four to six weeks old.

Kits **nurse** for the first nine to twelve weeks. Then they begin to hunt for food at night.

Scan this QR code to see kits in a tree!

★ Grown Raccoons ★

Raccoons are **independent** by one year old. Adult raccoons live alone or in small groups of four to five.

There are seven raccoon species. They **vary** in size. Some grow to 4 pounds (2 kg). Others can grow to 23 pounds (10 kg)!

All raccoon species **have** bushy tails with light **and** dark rings.

Good and grown!

★ Elder ★ Raccoons

Raccoons live up to five years in the wild. In captivity, they may live up to twenty years.

Raccoons have few **predators**. But they can be attacked by cougars, coyotes, and bobcats.

Disease and being hit by cars are raccoons' greatest threats.

Chapter 2

FORESTS & CITIES

Raccoons live around the world. Traditional raccoon **habitats** are forests near water.

Raccoons eat fish, frogs, eggs, fruit, insects, and nuts. But they will eat almost anything, including human garbage!

Raccoons sleep much of the day. They hunt and **forage** at night.

Scan this QR code to see a raccoon eating!

#NeatNickname
Raccoons are sometimes called "trash pandas"!

13

Today, many raccoons live in cities. They make homes in chimneys, attics, sewers, and more.

Raccoons' paws make them **adaptable**. Their front paws have five toes.

Raccoons use these much like human fingers.

Raccoons can grab, pull, and climb. They can also open jars and doorknobs!

#HandyHands
A raccoon's sensitive front paws help it identify food.

Raccoons are smart and **curious**. They have learned to **coexist** with people. For this reason, people have had many close encounters with raccoons.

Scan this QR code to see a sleepy raccoon!

Some people have captured these encounters! Silly raccoons charm the online world.

So do cute raccoons, sleepy raccoons, and playful raccoons!

Chapter 3

RACCOONS IN POP CULTURE

Raccoon content is all over the internet. But how and why did these clever creatures become social media stars?

Some animals become popular online because people think they're sweet. But raccoons are often seen as naughty.

They sneak into homes. They eat trash! Many people call raccoons pests. But others relate to them.

Some people think of raccoons as **underdogs**. They relate more to a scrappy animal than to pampered dogs or cats.

Raccoons are "verminfluencers." These animals are **vermin** that are loved online.

Some raccoons have even become social media celebrities!

★ Raccoon Royalty ★

Raccoon stars become famous in many ways. Some appear in a single meme. Others are featured on wildlife rescue social media accounts, websites, and more!

Superstar! MPR RACCOON

In June 2018, a raccoon climbed a twenty-five-story building in Minnesota. Minnesota Public Radio (MPR) posted raccoon photos and updates. The content went **viral**! People worldwide were relieved when the raccoon reached the building's roof. It was later released into the wild.

MEME BREAK!

TRYING TO LOOK COOL IN YOUR OLDER BROTHER'S HAND-ME-DOWNS

CLIMBING TO THE TOP OF THE JUNGLE GYM AND REALIZING YOU GOTTA CLIMB BACK DOWN

HOW IT FEELS SAYING GOODBYE TO CLASSMATES BEFORE SUMMER BREAK

WHEN MOM CATCHES ME IN THE FRIDGE AFTER SHE TOLD ME TO WAIT FOR DINNER

THAT FEELING WHEN YOU'RE IN CLASS LOOKING OUT THE WINDOW AT SCHOOLMATES WHO HAVE RECESS

RACCOONS ROCK!

Online raccoon love has spread offline! Raccoon characters appear on clothing, school supplies, and more.

Some people even keep raccoons as pets. But animal experts warn against this. Raccoons should live in the wild.

Internet fame has helped raccoons. It has led more people to protect raccoons and their wild habitats.

#Radcoon

adaptable: able to change depending on the situation

antic: a funny action that is meant to draw attention

coexist: to live together peacefully

content: ideas, facts, and images available online

curious: wanting to know more about something

forage: to search for food

habitat: where an animal lives

independent: not relying on others for support

nurse: to drink milk from a mother's body

predator: an animal that eats other animals to survive

underdog: something that is not perceived as having power

vary: to be different

viral: spreading quickly to many people over the internet

vermin: wild animals that are believed to be harmful or carry disease

WEBSITES

CBC Kids—8 Facts About Raccoons
https://www.cbc.ca/kidscbc2/the-feed/8-facts-about-raccoons
Check out eight cool raccoon facts, each supported by a photo.

The Kid Should See This—Raccoon Baby Rescue, Rehydration, and Reunion
https://thekidshouldseethis.com/post/30385625291
Watch a video and read about a baby raccoon that humans saved after it was trapped in a home chimney.

National Geographic Kids—Raccoons
https://kids.nationalgeographic.com/animals/mammals/raccoon/
Explore basic facts about raccoons through text, photos, and a map.

BOOKS

Downer, Ann. *Wild Animal Neighbors: Sharing Our Urban World.* Minneapolis: Twenty-First Century Books, 2014.
Learn why raccoons and other wildlife live in cities and how people can coexist with them.

Duhig, Holly. *Garbage and Trash.* Minneapolis: Lerner Publications, 2020.
Discover more about the diets of raccoons and other animals!

Riggs, Kate. *Raccoons.* Mankato, MN: Creative Education, 2017.
Dig into tons of raccoon info, including how the animals look and behave, where they live, and more.